# FRANKFURT

## BLICKE AUF DIE MAINMETROPOLE
## VIEWS OF THE MAIN METROPOLIS


bilder von andrea enderlein, fernando baptista, jochen günther

text von gabi winter

übersetzung barbara lynn



VERLAG

Bildnachweis:
Andrea Enderlein, Fernando Baptista, Jochen Günther

Gabi Winter
Frankfurt - Blicke auf die Mainmetropole


3. überarbeitete Auflage


Weitere Titel des B3 Verlages unter www.bedrei.de

Cover-Motiv: Jochen Günther

Druck und Bindung: Holtz AG, Neudrossenfeld

ISBN 3-938783-31-1

# inhalt/content

# frankfurt - 60 blicke auf eine pulsierende stadt

Typisch Frankfurt! Was ist das? Ist das der historische Römer, die "amerikanische" Skyline mit Banken- und Business-Riesen, Deutschlands Top-Flughafen, Grzimeks Zoo oder sind es die traditionellen und nachgewachsenen Ebbelwei-Viertel? Die 60 Blicke, die Andrea Enderlein, Fernando Baptista und Jochen Günther auf die Mainstadt geworfen haben, zeigen: Es gibt kein "entweder oder". Die kleinste Metropole der Welt beeindruckt durch grösstmögliche - und oft unerwartete - Vielfalt.

Wer in der City nur auf die um Superlative konkurrierenden Spitzen der Bankhochhäuser schaut, dem bleibt das Grün in den Tiefen der benachbarten Wallanlagen verschlossen. Frankfurt ist eben nicht nur "Bankfurt". Weitläufige Parks und Grünanlagen ziehen sich durch die gesamte Stadt. Alleine der Stadtwald umfasst nahezu 5000 Hektar. Und ist er “nur” eine Komponente des vielseitigen äußeren Grüngürtels, der - das haben Auszeichnungen der Vereinten Nationen und der UNESCO bekräftigt - beispielhafte Akzente für nachhaltige Stadtentwicklung und landschaftsbezogene Bildung setzt.

Wer lieber mit Vorurteilen lebt, übersieht auch: Die Mainmetropole musste sich nach den Zerstörungen im Zweiten Weltkrieg zwar in weiten Teilen neu erfinden, hat sich bis heute aber viel Ursprüngliches bewahrt. Der älteste Stadtteil Höchst zum Beispiel - übrigens nicht identisch mit der ehemaligen Hoechst AG, wie manche glauben - hat viel mehr zu bieten als Industrie und Chemie. Darunter eine malerische Altstadt, in der mit der Justinuskirche aus dem 9. Jahrhundert auch das älteste erhaltene Bauwerk der Stadt steht.

Es ist die Mischung aus innovativer wie zweckdienlicher Architektur, historisch erhaltenen und rekonstruierten Bauten, ausgedehnter Natur, 43 individuellen Stadtteilen und komplexen kulturellen Angeboten, die "Mainhattan" nicht nur für Frankfurter so einzigartig macht. Ländlich idyllische Wochenmärkte gehören ebenso zum Stadtbild wie das in den 1980er Jahren kreierte Museumsufer, an dem sich ein renommiertes Ausstellungshaus an das nächste reiht. Sehenswert sind nicht alleine berühmte Exponate aus Film, Architektur, Kunst, Kultur, Kommunikation, Stadt- und Weltgeschichte, sondern auch die Villen, die sie beherbergen.

Ebenso schnell wie das (Geschäfts-)Leben im finanzstarken Bankenviertel pulsiert, kommt es an den Ufern des Mains wieder zur Ruhe. Kaum ein Ort ist so sehr Sinnbild für die Wandelbarkeit der Stadt wie der weitgefächerte Raum um Frankfurts bedeutenden Fluss. Dort, wo früher Schlachthof, Strassen, Parkplätze und Industrieanlagen waren, geniessen heute Skater, Radfahrer und Spaziergänger ihre Freizeit. Frankfurt hat sich den Main als Ort zum Leben - und Feiern - zurückerobert.

Liebe auf den ersten Blick? Das fällt angesichts der Vielfalt und Kontraste, die Frankfurt bietet, schwer. Es ist ein Phänomen der nach Frankfurt Kommenden, dass sie der Stadt zunächst oft skeptisch begegnen, um sie nach näherem Kennenlernen umso dauerhafter zu lieben.

Die Mainmetropole will Schritt für Schritt entdeckt werden. Unsere Fotografen tragen mit ihren ganz persönlichen (An-)Sichten dazu bei. Ihre Bilder fangen Augenblicke einer lebendigen Stadt ein, die sich ihren Traditionen stellt, sich angesichts neuer An- und Herausforderungen aber auch stets weiterentwickelt. Zahlen von heute sind vielleicht morgen schon von gestern. Messestadt, Universitätsstadt, Einkaufsmetropole, Ausgehparadies - mal versnobt, mal bodenständig: Frankfurt ist eine Metropole mit vielen Facetten.

Menschen aus 180 Nationen, alle Frankfurter, prägen das Gesicht der Mainstadt entscheidend mit. "Multikulti", ein in dieser Stadt entstandener Begriff, wird hier auch im Alltag gelebt. Frankfurt empfängt die Welt nicht nur zu grossen Festen mit offenen Armen. Für manchen Fan kommt dabei die Liebe schon nach zehn, für andere auch erst nach 60 Blicken. +

# frankfurt - 60 views of a vibrant city

Typical Frankfurt? What is this? Is it the historic Römer, the "American" skyline with giant banks and businesses; is it Germany's leading airport, Grzimek's Zoo, or is it the traditional but expanded apple wine quarter?
The 60 viewpoints of the city on the Main which Andrea Enderlein, Fernando Baptista and Jochen Günther have recorded show that there is no need for choice. The smallest metropolis in the world impresses with its unsurpassed and often unexpected variety.

Anybody in the city who looks up only at the rival peaks of the tallest bank buildings misses the valleys of green just in their neighbourhood, formed by the embankments of the Anlage (city parks surrounding Frankfurt). Frankfurt is not just "Bankfurt". Extensive parks and green zones thread the whole city. The Stadtwald (city wood) - part of the outer Grüngürtel (green belt) - alone covers nearly 5.000 hectares and has been cited by the United Nations as a good example of sustainable landscape development.

Anyone who prefers to hold on to his prejudices will also fail to notice that the Main metropolis, despite the total destruction in the Second World War, has preserved much of its original feeling, while showing creativity in wide areas. For example Höchst, the oldest district in the city - by the way, not synonymous with the former Hoechst AG, as many believe - has much more to offer than industry and chemistry. This includes a picturesque old town, with the Justinus Church from the 9th century, which is also the oldest building of the city that has been preserved.

It is the mixture of functional and innovative architecture, historically preserved and reconstructed buildings, nature everywhere, 43 individual city districts, and a complex of cultural offerings, that make "Mainhattan" so unique, and that not only for the citizens of Frankfurt. Weekly markets reminiscent of rural idylls contribute to the city scene just as much as does the Museumsufer (Museum Embankment), created in the 1980s, where one famous gallery stands next to another. Not only the well-known exhibits from the worlds of film, architecture, art, culture, communication and the history of city and world are worth seeing, but also the villas which house them.

As fast as is the beat of (business) life in the financially strong banking quarter, just as fast comes the switch to peace on the banks of the River Main. Nothing symbolises better the chameleon character of the city than the wide spaces along Frankfurt's waterway. Where once a slaughterhouse, roads, car parks and industrial areas dominated, now skaters, cyclists and strollers enjoy themselves. Frankfurt has regained the Main as a place to live - and to celebrate.

Love at first sight? That is difficult to say, bearing in mind the variety and contrasts that Frankfurt offers. It is a phenomenon seen in those coming to Frankfurt for the first time, that they are initially sceptical and then on longer acquaintance come to love the city all the more deeply.

The Main Metropolis wants to be discovered in small steps. Our photographers contribute to that with their very personal view(point)s. Their pictures capture moments of a living city that is aware of its tradition but is always developing to meet new demands and challenges. What you count today can be already outdated tomorrow. Exhibition city, university city, shopping metropolis, paradise for evenings out - sometimes snobbish, sometimes down-to-earth: Frankfurt is a metropolis with many facets.

People from 180 nations, all however citizens of Frankfurt, are decisive in making up the face of the City on the Main. "Multikulti" (multicultural) is a word invented by this city, and is an everyday experience here. Frankfurt greets the world with open arms, and not only for big events. Some fans fall in love after 10 glances, some need 60.

# main

Kleine "Kreuzfahrten" sind auch auf Frankfurts grosser Wasserstrasse möglich. Auf die Schnelle zur historischen Gerbermühle und mit etwas mehr Zeit zur rheinischen Loreley. Fast wie auf der Autobahn: Auch hier trifft Urlaubs- auf Berufsverkehr. ✣

It is also possible to take short cruises along Frankfurt's main waterway: the historic Gerbermühle (leather curing mill) can be reached easily and quickly; with more time to spare, you can get to the Loreley, on the River Rhine. It is very similar to travelling on the autobahn, as here also, holiday and working traffic mingle. ✣

nationale suisse

**mainufer** Mit der Jolle vor Sonnenuntergang übers Wasser gleiten, im palmengesäumten "Nizza" einen Drink nehmen oder einfach von Hafen zu Hafen radeln: Frankfurt hat sich den Main nicht nur zum Wohnen, sondern auch als Freizeitparadies zurückerobert. ✤

Glide over the water before sunset in a dinghy, have a drink in the "Nizza" restaurant between palm trees, or simply row from one harbour to another: Frankfurt has reclaimed the Main for daily living and also as a leisure paradise. ✤

Rundfahrt

# mainbrücken

20 Brücken und Stege führen in Frankfurt per pedes, Auto, Zug oder Tram über den Main. Zentral gelegen, wetteifern der Eiserne Steg und der Holbeinsteg um die Gunst der Fußgänger, die zwischen "Dribbdebach" und "Hibbdebach" pendeln. +

Twenty bridges cross over the River Main in Frankfurt, for people on foot or in cars, trains or trams. Centrally placed, the Eisenersteg and the Holbeinsteg compete for the favour of pedestrians, who commute between " Dribbdebach" and "Hibbdebach". +

# osthafen

1912 eröffnet, ist der Osthafen, den im Jahr rund 1.800 Schiffe ansteuern, heute Arbeitsplatz für 2.500 Menschen. Nebenan, auf dem Gelände der früheren Großmarkthalle, entsteht der neue Hauptsitz der Europäischen Zentralbank EZB. ✢

The East Harbour, which opened in 1912, handles 1.800 ships every year. Today it employs 2.500 workers. Nearby the new headquarters of the European Central Bank (ECB) are rising on the site of the former Central Market. ✢

HFM Hafen Frankfurt
Managementgesellschaft mbH
D 9
KRAUSS MAFFEI
D 9

# alt-sachsenhausen

SAUER MACHT LUSTIG - UND GESELLIG. WER DAS FRANKFURTER "STÖFFCHE", DEN EBBELWEI, PROBIERT HAT, WEIß DAS AUS ERFAHRUNG. IN ALT-SACHSENHAUSEN STRÖMT ER SCHON SEIT "UR-ZEITEN" IN DIE BEMBEL. ✤

A GERMAN SAYING IS " SOUR MAKES LUSTY" - AND COMPANIABLE. IF YOU HAVE TRIED A GLASS OF FRANKFURT "DOPE" , EBBELWEI OR APPLE WINE, YOU KNOW THIS FROM EXPERIENCE. IN OLD SACHSENHAUSEN, IT HAS BEEN FLOWING SINCE TIMES GONE BY INTO THE LOCAL JUG, THE BEMBEL. ✤

Altes Haus
Warsteiner
EINE KÖNIGIN UNTER DEN BIEREN
Altes Haus
Bistro
Stern
GUINNESS
GUINNESS
GUINNESS
Coca-Cola
O2

KLAPPER

# portikus

Eine Maininsel ist die neue Heimat des Portikus, Ausstellungshalle für zeitgenössische Kunst. Das Gebäude mit lichtdurchflutetem Giebeldach wurde von Christoph Mäckler entworfen. ✤

An island in the River Main is the new home of Portikus, the exhibition centre for contemporary art. The building with its gabled roof, which lets light flood through, was designed by Christoph Mäckler. ✤

# walther-von-cronberg-platz

Dort, wo früher der Schlachthof stand, haben die Städteplaner den Traum vom Wohnen und Arbeiten am Fluss verwirklicht. Bauten wie das Main Plaza und das Colosseo geben dem Viertel ein völlig neues Gesicht. ✦ Here, on the site where the slaughterhouse once stood, the city planners have made the dream of living and working on the riverside a reality. Structures like the Main Plaza and the Colosseo have transformed the appearance of the district. ✦

LEÓN GARCIAS
Bitburger

# literaturhaus

Autorenlesungen, Ausstellungen und Gesprächsrunden zu zeitgenössischer Literatur sind "Programm" im klassizistischen Ambiente der Alten Stadtbibliothek. Ebenso wie Kinderbuch-Sonntage und die Schreibwerkstatt für Jugendliche. ✦

Readings by authors, exhibitions and talks on contemporary literature are on the programme in the classical ambience of the Old City Library. There are also Children's Book Sundays and writing workshops for young people. ✦

LITTERIS RECUPERATA LIBERTATE CIVITAS

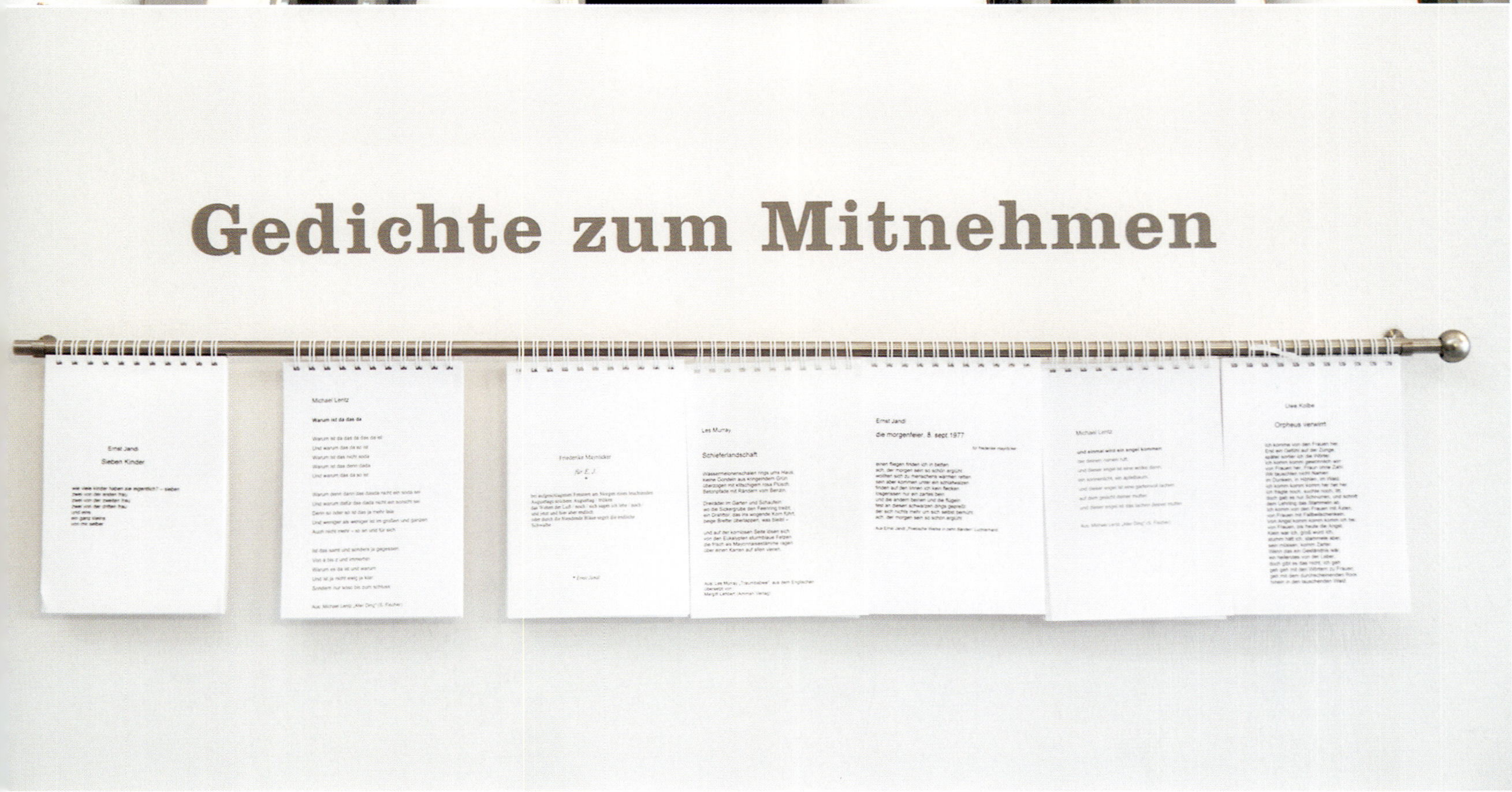
Gedichte zum Mitnehmen

# museumsuferfest

Mehr als drei Millionen Besucher zieht es jährlich zum Museumsuferfest, dem grössten Spektakel der Stadt. Ein gelungener Mix aus Kultur, Kunst, Unterhaltung und kulinarischen Genüssen aus aller Welt. ✦

The Museumsuferfest, Frankfurt's most spectacular event, attracts over 3 million visitors each year. A successful mix of culture, art, entertainment and culinary pleasures from all over the world. ✦

Hier gibt's
LANGOS
Ungarn!

## museumsufer

Etwa 60 Ausstellungshäuser gibt es in Frankfurt, grosse und kleine, alte wie neue. Besonders dicht und prächtig gewachsen ist diese beeindruckende Kulturlandschaft am Museumsufer. Mit ihrem harmonischen Ensemble von historischen und modernen Gebäuden bietet sie dort - auf kurzen Wegen - nicht nur im Deutschen Architekturmuseum städteplanerische Highlights. Am Schaumainkai residieren neben anderen namhaften Nachbarn das Museum für Angewandte Kunst, das Museum der Weltkulturen, das Deutsche Filmmuseum und das Museum für Kommunikation. ✦ There are around 60 museums and galleries in Frankfurt, large and small, old as well as new. The impressive cultural landscape along the Museumsufer (Museums Embankment) has grown particularly thickly and magnificently. With a harmonious ensemble of historic and modern buildings, it offers within a short distance highlights of (town) planning - and not only in the Deutschen Architekturmuseum (German Museum of Architecture). Residing on the Schaumainkai are the Museum für Angewandte Kunst (Museum of Applied Art), the Museum der Weltkulturen (Museum of World Cultures), the Deutsches Filmmuseum (German Film Museum) and the Museum für Kommunication (Communication Museum) next to other equally famous neighbours. ✦

AUGENBLICKE
KERAMIK DER MOCHE UND SHIPIBO-PERU

# das städel

**LEBENDIG.** ✣ HIER WERDEN ALTE MEISTER SELBST FÜR DEN NACHWUCHS ZUM ERLEBNIS: IN WELTBERÜHMTEN GEMÄLDEN, GRAFIKEN UND SKULPTUREN BLEIBEN DIE SIEBEN JAHRHUNDERTE UMFASSENDEN ERFAHRUNGSWELTEN BEDEUTENDER EUROPÄISCHER KÜNSTLER LEBENDIG. ✣

HERE THE OLD MASTERS THEMSELVES CAN BE EXPERIENCED BY THE YOUNGER GENERATION. IN WORLD-FAMOUS PAINTINGS, DRAWINGS AND SCULPTURES THE WORLDS OF SEVEN CENTURIES OF MAJOR EUROPEAN ARTISTS REMAIN ALIVE. ✣

# liebieghaus

Renommierte Bildhauerkunst von der Antike bis zum Klassizismus, präsentiert in einer imposanten Villa mit erlesenem Park: Das Museum Alter Plastik bietet in mehr als einer Hinsicht Sehenswertes. ✣ Famous sculptures from antique to classical can be seen in this imposing villa, set in a very special park. The Museum of old Sculptures offers much that is worth seeing from several perspectives. ✣

# flohmarkt

Sammler, Heimwerker, Schnäppchen- und Antiquitätenjäger aufgepasst: Das Dorado für Secondhand-Freaks liegt samstags am Museumsufer. Ganz gleich, ob zum Feilschen, Stöbern oder Klönen. +

Look out collectors, do-it-yourselfers and hunters for bargains and antiques: the El Dorado for those who can't resist a second-hand bargain can be found on the Museumsufer every Saturday. No matter whether you want to haggle, to rummage or to chat. +

# historische innenstadt

Wer ein wenig über den "Tellerrand" des Römerbergs hinausschaut, entdeckt schnell noch weitere historische Schätze. Die um 1160 erbaute Palastkapelle des bis zu den Staufern zurückreichenden Saalhofs - inzwischen Teil des Historischen Museums - gilt als eines der ältesten Bauwerke der Stadt. Schiffsleute entrichteten im benachbarten "Rententurm", 1456 erbaut, die fälligen Gebühren. Im "Steinernen Haus" der Patrizierfamilie Melem werden heute zahlende Gäste zu Tisch gebeten. ✣

If you move away from the well-trodden paths of the Römerberg, you very soon discover further historical treasures. The palace chapel of the Saalhof, itself reaching back to Staufen times and now part of the Historical Museum, was built around 1160 and is thought to be one of the oldest buildings in the city. Sailors paid their dues in the adjacent "Rententurm" tower, built in 1456. The Steinernes Haus (Stone House) of the Melems, a patrician family, now bids paying guests to meals. ✣

# römerberg

Auch wenn aus dem Gerechtigkeitsbrunnen nunmehr Wasser statt Wein fliesst und die historischen Fachwerkhäuser zwar stilecht, aber nicht mehr als Originale vorhanden sind, ist und bleibt der Römerberg Frankfurts "Gudd Stubb". Hier wusste das Volk schon immer zu feiern. Ob Kaiserkrönung im Dom oder der Empfang triumphierender Sportidole auf dem Balkon des Römers: An geeigneten Anlässen hat es in der facettenreichen Geschichte der Mainstadt noch nie gemangelt. ✦

Although water now flows from the Fountain of Justice instead of wine, and the historic half-timbered houses look authentic but are not the originals, the Römerberg itself is still Frankfurt's "Gudd Stubb". This is where the people of Frankfurt have always known how to celebrate. Whether for the coronation of the Emperor in the Cathedral or greeting victorious sporting idols on the balcony overlooking the Römer, the multi-facetted city on the Main has never been lacking in suitable opportunities. ✦

CASH-SERVICE
GELD- UND
WECHSELSTUBE
KAFFEE
CHANGE
Renate Bamberg

# römer

HIER WIRD SEIT MEHR ALS 600 JAHREN POLITIK GEMACHT UND (STADT-)GESCHICHTE GESCHRIEBEN. DER RÖMER, NACH DEM "MUTTERHAUS" DES RATHAUSKOMPLEXES BENANNT, IST NICHT NUR IM KAISERSAAL REPRÄSENTATIVER TREFFPUNKT FÜR GEKRÖNTE UND UNGEKRÖNTE HÄUPTER. ✣

HERE, POLICY HAS BEEN MADE AND (CITY) HISTORY WRITTEN FOR MORE THAN 600 YEARS. THE RÖMER, NAMED AFTER THE "MOTHER HOUSE" OF THE TOWN HALL COMPLEX, IS AN IMPOSING MEETING PLACE FOR LEADERS, WHETHER KINGS OR COMMONERS, AND NOT ONLY IN THE KAISERSAAL. ✣

karl·iv·

# alte nikolaikirche

KÖNIGLICHE HOFKIRCHE, ZENTRUM DER ALMOSENPFLEGE UND RATSKAPELLE: DIE GESCHICHTE DER ÄLTESTEN EVANGELISCHEN GEMEINDEKIRCHE FRANKFURTS REICHT BIS INS MITTELALTER ZURÜCK. IHR 47-STIMMIGES GLOCKENSPIEL ERKLINGT DREIMAL TÄGLICH ÜBER DEM RÖMERBERG. ✦

COURT CHURCH, CENTRE FOR CHARITABLE WORKS AND COUNCIL CHAPEL: THE HISTORY OF THE OLDEST PROTESTANT CHURCH IN FRANKFURT REACHES BACK TO THE MIDDLE AGES. ITS 47-CHIME GLOCKENSPIEL RINGS OUT OVER THE RÖMERBERG 3 TIMES A DAY. ✦

# das alte rathaus

Ob zugekaufte Bürgerhäuser oder historische Rathaus-Neubauten: Ein einheitliches Gebilde ist der Römer - im Laufe der Jahrhunderte mit den Aufgaben seiner Bediensteten gewachsen - beileibe nicht. Das "jüngste" Gebäude entstand, zweiteilig, um 1900. Im Nordbau am Paulsplatz werden damals wie heute die städtischen Finanzen verwaltet. Grund genug für Bürger, die zur Kasse gebeten wurden, den Übergang vom Südbau - unter anderem Domizil des malerischen Ratskellers - die "Seufzerbrücke" zu nennen. ✣

Whether dwelling houses purchased from citizens or the new town hall building, itself now historic: the Römer is in no way a unified structure. It has just grown over the centuries with the work of its civil servants. The "newest" building - with two sections - dates from 1900. The north building on the Paulsplatz ( St Paul's Square) has always been the home of the city's financial administration, a good reason for citizens who were required to pay their debts, to call the crossing from the south building - also the location of the picturesque Ratskeller (town hall restaurant) - the Bridge of Sighs. ✣

# kaiserdom

Seit 1356 Wahlkirche der deutschen Könige, wurde St. Bartholomäus von 1562 bis 1792 gar Krönungsstätte der hiesigen Kaiser. Für die Frankfurter ist ihre grösste Pfarrkirche deshalb der Dom - auch wenn sie nie Bischofssitz war. ✣

St. Bartholomew, the electoral church of the German kings since 1356, was even the location for the coronation of the Holy Roman Emperor between 1562 and 1792. For Frankfurt citizens their largest parish church is therefore called the Cathedral, even if it has never been the seat of a bishop. ✣

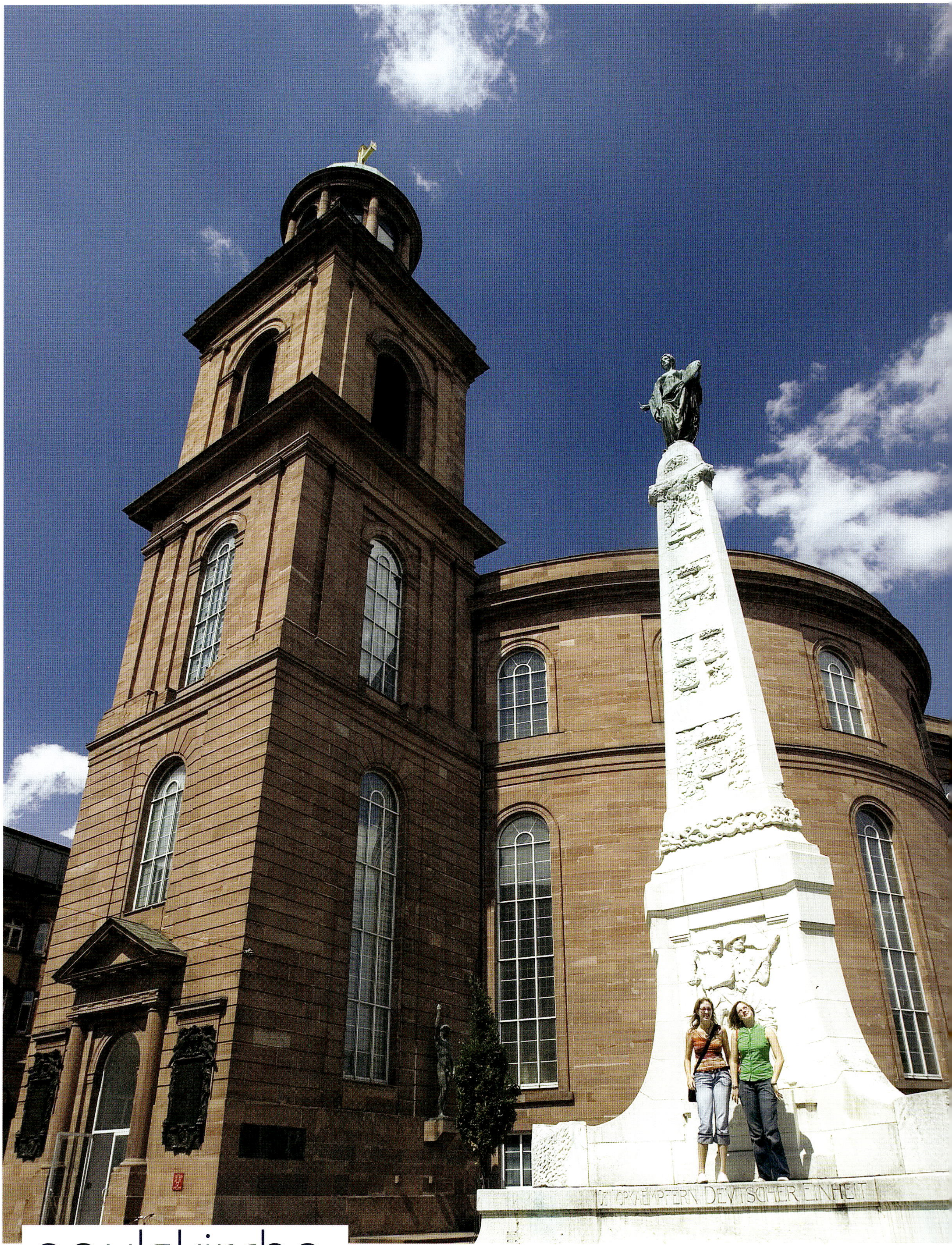


# paulskirche

1848 nahm das erste frei gewählte deutsche Parlament - die Nationalversammlung - in der Paulskirche seine Arbeit auf. Wandgemälde und Ausstellungen legen bis heute in der "Wiege der deutschen Demokratie" davon Zeugnis ab. ✣

In 1848 the first freely-elected German parliament - the National Assembly - took up its work in St Paul's Church. Murals and exhibitions in the " cradle of German democracy" testify to this up to the present day. ✣

DIE EROBERUNG DER STRASSE

# karmeliterkloster

Engagierte Ordensleute prägen das soziale Leben in der Mainmetropole sichtbar mit. Das frühere Karmeliterkloster zeigt: Diese Tradition reicht bis ins Mittelalter zurück. Hier ist heute das Museum für Vor- und Frühgeschichte untergebracht. ✣

The commitment of members of religious orders made a visible impact on the community life of the Main-Metropolis. The former Carmelite Cloister shows that this tradition goes back to the Middle Ages. Today the Museum of Pre- and Early History is housed here. ✣

# die warten

Im 15. Jahrhundert erbaut, trugen sie dazu bei, unerwünschte Eindringlinge in ihre Grenzen zu verweisen: der Eschenheimer Turm als Teil der Stadtmauer, Bockenheimer-, Sachsenhäuser-, Friedberger- und Gallus-Warte gehörten zur Landwehr. ✣ Built in the 15th century, they helped to drive unwelcome intruders back to their borders: the Eschenheimer Turm as part of the city wall, while the Bockenheim, Sachsenhausen, Friedberg and Gallus watchtowers were territorial defences. ✣

FRIEDBERGER WARTE

# börse

Wer Börsenmaklern beim Jonglieren mit Zahlen über die Schulter schauen möchte, kommt an "Bulle und Bär" nicht vorbei. Die neue Konzernzentrale der Deutschen Börse ist zwar nach Eschborn umgezogen, rund sieben Kilometer von der Franfurter Innenstadt entfernt. Der Parketthandel von Deutschlands bedeutendster Wertpapierbörse wird aber nach wie vor im feudalen Haus in der City abgewickelt. +

If you would like to look over the shoulder of brokers while they are busy juggling their figures, don't pass the "Bull and Bear". Although the Corporate Headquarters moved to Eschborn, seven kilometres from the city center, Germany's most important stock exchange has its trading floor still in the magnificent building in the city. +

BÖRSE FRANKFURT

Frankfurter Allgemeine
Börsen-Zeitung
FINANCIAL TIMES
DIE ZEIT

# goethe-haus

Auch wenn es ihn später nach Weimar zog, Johann Wolfgang von Goethe bleibt Frankfurts berühmtester Kopf. Im Grossen Hirschgraben wurde er 1749 geboren. Das Haus ist zwar nicht mehr im Original erhalten, wurde aber stilecht rekonstruiert. ✦ Although life took him later to Weimar, Goethe remains Frankfurt's most famous person. He was born in 1749 in Grossen Hirschgraben. Little remains now of the original house but it has been authentically reconstructed ✦

# frankfurter hof

Nach außen holt er den Glanz kaiserlicher Zeiten in die City zurück, innen verwöhnt er mit modernem Komfort. Der Steigenberger Frankfurter Hof - eines der namhaftesten Hotels der Welt - ist seit 1876 eine Institution in Frankfurt. Durch den Bombenhagel 1944 zerstört, wurde er in den Nachkriegsjahren in alter Pracht wieder aufgebaut und ist heute denkmalgeschützt. Sein elegantes Flair ist nicht nur bei internationalen Gästen beliebt, sondern - unter anderem - auch bei einheimischen Grössen. ✦ From the outside it brings the brilliance of imperial times back to the city. Inside, it indulges visitors with modern comfort. The Steigenberger Frankfurter Hof - one of the most famous hotels in the world - has been a Frankfurt institution since 1876. Destroyed in the devastating bombing raids of 1944, it was rebuilt in all its old splendour in the years after the war and is now a protected historical monument. Its elegant flair is popular not only with international guests but also with, among others, local celebrities. ✦

MTX UL 858
MTX RR 771

STEIGENBERGER FRANKFURTER HOF
Friedensstraße

# hauptbahnhof

Täglich eilen oder verweilen hier rund 350.000 Reisende und Besucher. Auf keinem anderen deutschen Bahnhof legen so viele Fernreise-Züge im selben Zeitraum einen Stopp ein. Das historische Gebäude ist dabei mehr als einen Blick wert. Übrigens auch für diejenigen, die nicht deutschland- und europaweit unterwegs sind, sondern nur eine schnelle Verbindung innerhalb der Region oder der Mainmetropole suchen. +

Around 350,000 travellers and visitors daily rush through here, or linger a while. In a given period of time, more long-distance trains make a stop here than in any other German station. The historic building itself is then worth more than just a glance. This also applies, by the way, to those who are not in the course of journeys across Germany and Europe but only want to catch a quick regional or city connection +

# bahnhofsviertel

Die schmucke Kaiserstrasse gehört ebenso zu Frankfurts zweitkleinstem Stadtteil wie das benachbarte Rotlicht-Milieu. Mit ihrer Mischung aus Sex and Crime sind Teile des Viertels auch Kulisse für manchen Krimi. ✣ The smart Kaiserstrasse belongs to Frankfurt's second smallest district just as much as does the neighbouring red-light area. Offering a mixture of sex and crime, parts of the quarter are also used as the scene for many a thriller. ✣

CRAZY SEXY
CRAZY
SEXY

# westhafen

Der 112 Meter hohe Westhafen-Tower, im Volksmund "Das Gerippte" (= Apfelweinglas) genannt, ist Wahrzeichen des neuen Wohn- und Büroviertels am Westhafen. Yachten und Boote bringen einen Hauch von Riviera an den Main. ✣

The 112-metre high Westhafen tower, popularly called " Das Gerippte" (name of the traditional glass for apple wine) is the symbol of the new residential and office quarter at the west harbour. Yachts and other boats bring a Riviera breeze to the Main. ✣

# skyline

Hoch, höher, am höchsten. Das Wolkenkratzer-Ensemble von "Mainhattan" ist in Europa einzigartig. Wen stört's, dass ein Moskauer Turm den Commerzbank-Tower (259 Meter) inzwischen überholte? ✦

High, higher, highest: the skyscraper ensemble of "Mainhattan" is unique in Europe. Who worries that a tower in Moscow has overtaken the Commerzbank tower (259 metres)? ✦

# mainzer landstrasse

Tradition trifft auf Moderne, Geld auf Kultur. Nahe der Alten Oper schiessen die Bürotürme grosser Banken und Konzerne in die Höhe. Die Chaussee von einst mischt heute im Bankenviertel mit. ✣

Tradition encounters modernity, money meets culture. Near the Alte Oper the office towers of major banks and businesses shoot up in the sky. What was once the high road to Frankfurt is now integrated into the banking quarter. ✣

DEM WAHREN SCHOENEN GUTEN

# messeturm

Der 256,5 Meter hohe "Bleistift" ist Wahrzeichen der Messe der Stadt Frankfurt. Zu seinen Füßen der "Hammering Man", der signalisiert: Hier stehen die Geschäfte nie still. ✣ The 265.5-metre high Trade Fair Tower - the "pencil" - is the symbol of the Frankfurt city Trade Fair. At its feet, the "Hammering Man", signals that "here business never stands still". ✣

# messe

Das Frankfurter Messegelände - weltweit das drittgrößte - ist Schauplatz für rund 50 Messen und Ausstellungen pro Jahr. Darunter Klassiker wie Internationale Buchmesse, Ambiente und IAA, die Gäste aus allen Erdteilen in die Stadt bringen. ✦

The Frankfurt exhibition grounds - the third largest in the world - are the scene for around 50 fairs and exhibitions each year. Among them, classics like the International Book Fair, Ambiente and the International Motor Show, which bring guests to the city from all quarters of the globe. ✦

# bürostadt niederrad

Diese "Stadt in der Stadt" hat zwei Gesichter. Tagsüber pulsiert in den seit Jahrzehnten gewachsenen Bürohäusern das Geschäftsleben, abends - wenn Zehntausende von Pendlern das Viertel verlassen - kehrt Stille ein. +

This "city within the city" has two faces. During the day business life vibrates in the office blocks built within the last ten years. In the evening when tens of thousands of commuters have left the quarter, peace returns. +

Einbahnstraße
ATRICOM

# schwanheim

Altes Fachwerk, begrünte Innenhöfe oder die auch als "Dom des Maingau" bekannte Mauritiuskirche: All das macht den Charme von Schwanheim - im Jahr 880 erstmals als Bauerndorf "Sueinheim" erwähnt - bis heute aus. Für Grossstädter ebenso wichtig: das Naturschutzgebiet "Schwanheimer Düne" und der Spielpark im Stadtwald. Dort lässt es sich nicht nur zu Eulenspiegels Füssen herrlich planschen. ✣

Old half-timbered houses, nicely-planted courtyards or the Church of St. Maurice, also known as the Cathedral of the Rheingau: all these comprise the charm of Schwanheim today, first documented in 880 as the farming village "Sueinheim". Equally important for city-dwellers: the nature reserve "Schwanheimer Düne" (Schwanheim Dunes) and the playground in the Stadwald (city wood). It's not only at the feet of Till Eulenspiegel that one can splash around there. ✣

# höchst

Die Altstadt ist denkmalgeschützt, rund ums Schloss - einst Residenz der Mainzer Erzbischöfe - feiern die Höchster tolle Feste. Mehr als einen Abstecher wert: der idyllische Bolongarogarten. ✣

The old town is an historic monument; around the Schloss, once the residence of the Archbishop of Mainz, the people of Höchst now celebrate their feastdays. The idyllic Bolangaro garden is worth more than just a brief visit. ✣

Schwan
Zum Schwan
Zum Bären
Alte Zollwache

## flughafen

Bei der Luftfracht liegt er in Europa mit über zwei Millionen Tonnen Fracht im Jahr längst auf Platz 1, in Sachen Passagiere muss Frankfurts Airport mit annähernd 53 Millionen (2006) nur London und Paris den Vorrang lassen. Durch den geplanten Ausbau könnten im Jahr 2020 prognostizierte 88 Millionen Fluggäste befördert werden. Für die Menschen aus der Region ist "ihr Flughafen" schon heute viel mehr als ein weltweit bedeutender Verkehrsknotenpunkt. Als "Stadt in der Stadt" bietet er auch die zugehörige Infrastruktur mit mannigfaltigen Einkaufsmöglichkeiten, Restaurants, Klinik, Kapelle, modernen Bahnhöfen und - last, not least - rund 70.000 Arbeitsplätzen. + While ranking as the number one cargo airport in Europe with over two million tons of airfreight per year, as a passenger airport, Frankfurt airport with its nearly 53 million passengers (in 2006) is surpassed only by London and Paris. The intended airport extension project would prospectively permit 88 million travellers to be handled by 2020. For people in the region, the airport is already a lot more than an important international junction. As a "city within the city" it offers the appropriate infrastructure with a large variety of shopping facilities, restaurants, a clinic, a chapel, modern railway stations , and - last but not least - around 70.000 jobs. +

AIR BERLIN

# commerzbank-arena

Bei Heim-Spielen der Eintracht wird's den Fußball-Fans hier richtig heiß. Garantiert auf dem Siedepunkt ist die Stimmung auch, wenn die Rolling Stones oder Genesis in dem Stadion rocken, das wegen seines innovativen Dachs als "größtes Cabrio der Welt" gefeiert wird. +

Emotions run high when football club Eintracht Frankfurt holds its home matches here. And the sizzling atmosphere reaches its peak when the Rolling Stones or Genesis perform at "the world's largest convertible", as the stadium has been nicknamed on account of its innovative roof structure. +

Licher
AVIS

# goetheturm

196 Stufen muss man erklimmen, um im Stadtwald zum Aussichtspunkt des 43 Meter hohen Goetheturms zu gelangen. Der Blick, den man bei gutem Wetter über Frankfurt, bis hin zu Taunus, Spessart und Odenwald erhält, entschädigt für die Mühen. Die Kleinen haben auch ohne derartige Anstrengungen viel Spass. Im Waldspielpark zu Füssen des hölzernen "Giganten" warten Spielgeräte und ein Planschbecken auf sie. Neueste Attraktion ist ein Irrgarten, der kleine und große Entdecker zum wasserspendenden Grüngürteltier führt. ✦

Visitors have to conquer 196 steps to reach the viewing platform of the 43-metres-high Goethe Tower, in the city-wood (Stadtwald). The view, which in good weather stretches beyond Frankfurt, to the Taunus, Spessart and Odenwald, compensates for the effort. Small visitors can also have fun, without such exertions. Playground equipment and a paddling pool are waiting for them in the Woodland Playpark, at the foot of the wooden "giant ". The most recent attraction is a maze, which leads small and large explorers to a water-spouting "Grüngürteltier", the animal symbol of Frankfurt's green belt. ✦

BINDING

# parks

Frankfurt blüht auf - inmitten heimischer Gewächse ebenso wie in exotischen Pavillons. Mehr als 50 Parks und Anlagen bringen die Natur, über die Stadt verteilt, fast vor die "Haustür". ✣

In local gardens as much as in pavilions with exotic displays, Frankfurt is in bloom. Across the city, in more than 50 parks and other green spaces, Nature is brought up to the front door. ✣

# alter jüdischer friedhof

Der Alte Jüdische Friedhof an der Battonstrasse, im 13. Jahrhundert erstmals erwähnt, zeugt von der eng mit Frankfurt verbundenen jüdischen Geschichte. Einst standen 6.500 Grabsteine auf diesem zweitältesten jüdischen Friedhof Deutschlands, rund 4.000 davon wurden 1943 durch die Nationalsozialisten zerstört. Mehr als 11.000 in die Friedhofsmauer eingelassene Gedenksteine erinnern an die während der NS-Zeit aus Frankfurt verschleppten und ermordeten jüdischen Mitbürger der Stadt. ✦

The Old Jewish Cemetery in Battonstrasse, first documented in the 13th century, gives testimony to the history of the Jewish population of Frankfurt, closely linked with that of the city. Originally 6,500 headstones stood in this, the second-oldest Jewish cemetery in Germany; however about 4,000 of these were destroyed by the National Socialists in 1943. More than 11,000 memorial tablets set in the cemetery wall recall the Jewish citizens of the city, deported and murdered while the National Socialists were in power. ✦

IRENE ROSENTHAL
28.12.1921
AUSCHWITZ

# anlagenring

Hochhausschluchten umgeben von viel Grün und Kunst - Frankfurt fasziniert mit Kontrasten. In der Taunusanlage, Teil des innerstädtischen Anlagenrings, machen auch Banker gerne Pause. ✦

Canyons between skyscrapers surrounded by plentiful greenery and art: Frankfurt has fascinating contrasts. In the Taunusanlage, part of the inner city green belt, even bankers are happy to take a break ✦

## ZOO

Bernhard Grzimek begründete den Weltruf des Frankfurter Zoos. Camp und Flieger erinnern die Besucher an seine Serengeti-Expeditionen. In der Beliebtheitsskala ungeschlagen sind jedoch Raubkatzen, Gorillas, Nashorn & Co. +

Bernhard Grzimek laid the foundation of Frankfurt Zoo's worldwide reputation. Campsite and aeroplane remind the visitor of his Serengeti expedition. Despite this, big cats, gorillas, rhino and co. are unbeaten in the popularity scale. +

# palmengarten

Im tropischen Dschungel untertauchen, lebende Steine und "Fleischfresser" bestaunen oder gemütlich relaxen: Der Palmengarten, 1868 gegründet, macht's zum - natürlichen - Grossstadt-Erlebnis. ✦ Disappear into a tropical jungle, marvel at living stones and carnivorous plants or just relax in comfort: the Palmengarten, founded in 1868, has become - in a natural way - a big city experience. ✦

# museum für moderne kunst

Wo begegnet Andy Warhols Pop Art kunstvoll gestalteten Objekten von Joseph Beuys? Im grössten "Tortenstück" Frankfurts: Dort warten wahre Leckerbissen zeitgenössischer Kunst auf die Besucher. +

Where does the Pop Art of Andy Warhol meet the artfully created objects of Josef Beuys? In Frankfurt's largest "slice of cake": there the delicacies offered the visitor are among the best of contemporary art.

# schirn kunsthalle

Ausstellungen, die alle Epochen und Stilrichtungen umfassen, zum Schauen und Diskutieren einladen, Künstler von Weltruf präsentieren, bescheren der Schirn ein Millionen-Publikum. Ihr Ruf reicht weit über Deutschlands Grenzen hinaus. ✦

The exhibitions which the Schirn brings to its one million public encompass all periods and styles. Inviting observation and discussion, they present artists of international renown. Its reputation reaches far beyond Germany's borders. ✦

SCHIRNKUNSTHALLE

# zeil/hauptwache

Hier wird richtig Umsatz gemacht: Zwischen Konstablerwache und Hauptwache - einst legendäres Gefängnis, heute beliebtes Café - liegt Frankfurts Einkaufsmeile Nummer 1. Ein gesuchter Standort für alle grossen Kaufhäuser der Republik. ✦

This is where the turnover is: Frankfurt's Number 1 Shopping Mile lies between Konstablerwache and Hauptwache - once a legendary prison, today a popular café. A sought-after location for all of Germany's large department stores. ✦

ESPRIT
HAKO

# frankfurt bei nacht

... ist für sich genommen schon ein Erlebnis. Licht- und Bilderspektakel wie die "Luminale" und die phänomenale "SkyArena" zum Auftakt der Fußball-WM sorgen für Gänsehaut-Feeling pur.

... is now an experience in its own right. Illumination and picture spectaculars like the "Luminale" and the phenomenal "SkyArena" at the start of the World Cup create that special thrill.

# nightlife

Techno, Jazz, Funk, Blues: Im prallen Nachtleben der Mainmetropole gibt es nichts, was es nicht gäbe. Ob in der stylishen Bar oder der schrillen Disco: Langweilig wird's weder auf High-Heels noch in Sneakers. ✤

Techno, Jazz, Funk, Blues: in the packed nightlife of the Main - Metropolis, every possibility can be found. Whether in a stylish bar or a shrill disco, on high-heels or in sneakers, you will never be bored. ✤

# märkte

"Aale Worscht" ganz frisch oder ein gutes "Stöffche" direkt vom Erzeuger? Dafür fahren die Frankfurter nicht aufs Land, das "Land" kommt zu ihnen. Ob in der City oder den Stadtteilen: Mindestens einmal die Woche ist Markttag. +

Fresh "Aale Worscht" (sausage) or good "Stöffche" (a drink) direct from the producer? To get these, Frankfurt's citizens needn't journey to the country: the country journeys to them. A market is held at least once a week, in the city and in each of the suburbs. +

BOHNEN
eingelegt
100gr .... 1,30
PEPERONI
MILD
100gr .. 1,30
AUBERGINEN
SALAT
100gr ... 2,60
TARAMA
SALAT
100gr ... 2,30
SCHAFSKASE
eingelegt
100gr ... 2,40
SCHAFSKASE
- NATUR -
100gr ... 1,80
POMODORI
- STÜCKE
ZITRONEN
OLIVEN
100gr ... 1,40
KAPERN-
BEEREN
100gr ... 2,00
PEPERONI
eingelegt
100gr ... 1,50
KAPERN
ARTISCHOKEN
LEISURE TIME

# brunnen

HISTORISCH, HUMORIG, KLASSISCH, MODERN ODER EINFACH NUR ERFRISCHEND NASS: 145 BRUNNEN - PRIVATE NICHT MITGEZÄHLT - SCHMÜCKEN DIE STADT. VIELE DAVON ERZÄHLEN FRANKFURTER GESCHICHTE(N). UNTER ANDEREM VON STRUWWELPETER, MERKUR, JUSTITIA UND FRAU RAUSCHER. DIE "VERSPRÜHT" IHREN CHARME IN SACHSENHAUSEN, WO MAN IN ALTER TRADITION IM SOMMER DAS GROßE BRUNNENFEST FEIERT. ✤ HISTORICAL, AMUSING, CLASSICAL, MODERN, OR JUST REFRESHINGLY WET - THE CITY IS ENHANCED BY 145 FOUNTAINS AND WELLS, NOT COUNTING THE PRIVATE ONES. MANY OF THEM TELL THE TALES AND HISTORY OF FRANKFURT, OF SLOVENLY PETER, MERCURY, LADY JUSTICE AND MRS. RAUSCHER, WHO SPLASHES WATER IN SACHSENHAUSEN, WHERE THE TRADITIONAL FOUNTAIN FESTIVAL ("BRUNNENFEST") IS CELEBRATED EVERY SUMMER. ✤

Die Frau Rauscher
aus de Klappergaß,
die hot e Beul am Ei.
Ob's vom Rauscher,
ob's vom Alte kimmt,
das klärt die Polizei.
Francofur

# shopping

Zum Frühstück bei Tiffany's muss "Frau" nicht nach New York fliegen, für die Juwelen von Cartier kann man(n) sich die Fahrt nach Paris sparen. Sehen und gesehen werden, edelste Ware in den Schaufenstern, das hält die Mainmetropole in der Goethestrasse bereit. Im Gegensatz zu den vielen Prachtboulevards dieser Welt läuft sich hier niemand die Füsse wund, bis er mit vollen Einkaufstaschen heimkehrt. Nobelmarken wie Chanel, Versace und Mont Blanc residieren auf wenigen hundert Metern Tür an Tür. Weniger prall gefüllt darf der Geldbeutel für die Shopping-Tour in den Stadtteilen sein. In der Schweizer Strasse oder der Berger Strasse gibt's gefragte Marken auch schon mal als Secondhand-Schnäppchen - und den Capuccino "open air" dazu.

For breakfast at Tiffanys, women don't have to fly to New York. For jewels from Cartier, men can save themselves the trip to Paris. See and be seen, an exquisite selection of goods in the shop windows, that's what the Main-Metropolis offers in the Goethestrasse. Top brands like Chanel, Versace and Montblanc are to be found door to door in just a few hundred metres. To shop in other parts of the city, you don't need such a well-filled purse. You can find what you are looking for in the Schweizer Strasse or the Berger Strasse, sometimes even as a secondhand bargain, and with a Capuccino in an open-air café as well.

TIFFANY & CO.
TIFFANY & CO.

BOGNER
GIORGIO ARMANI

29
MONT BLANC
MONT BLANC

# kleinmarkthalle

Vielfalt für Augen, Nase und Gaumen entfaltet die Kleinmarkthalle für alle, die gerne kochen oder bekocht werden. Ob Zutaten fürs "Rippche" mit Kraut oder doch eher fürs Couscous: Das Angebot an frischer Ware ist wie die Stadt - multikulturell. ✤

The Kleinmarkthalle unfolds variety for the eyes, nose and palate of anyone who takes pleasure in cooking or being cooked for. Whether ingredients for "Rippche mit Kraut" (smoked pork with cabbage ) or more probably for couscous, the range of fresh produce offered is like the city - multicultural. ✤

Caviar Galerie
Kürbiskerne -naturell-
Pinienkerne -naturell-
Macadamia -leichgeröstet-
Persische Pistazien -H. Naturell-
Persische Pistazien -H.wenigersalz-
Persische Pistazien

# fressgass

Die "Fressgass" - eigentlich Grosse Bockenheimer Strasse - macht ihrem Namen alle Ehre. In den Schaufenstern drapierte Delikatessen sind echte Highlights für Gourmets und Gourmands. Selbstverständlich kann man in den Genusstempeln der Fussgänger-Zone auch à la carte bestellen. Rund 400.000 Besucher kommen jährlich zum beliebten Rheingauer Weinmarkt auf die Flaniermeile. ✦

The "Fressgass ", literally "Eating Street " and actually Grosse Bockenheimer Strasse, does its name justice. In shop windows the beautiful arrangement of delicacies is a true highlight for gourmets and gourmands. Naturally you can also order from the menu in the pedestrian area's temples of pleasure. Around 400,000 visitors come yearly to the popular Rheingau Wine Market on this street for sauntering. ✦

37-39
China
Restaurant
Jasmin

Schlemmermeyer
Schlemmermeyer
eterna
MAREDO

# weihnachtsmarkt

Alle Jahre wieder... zieht es rund drei Millionen Besucher von nah und fern auf den Frankfurter Weihnachtsmarkt. Nikolaus, Lichterglanz und Glühwein gibt's auch in anderen Metropolen, Goethes geliebte Brenten und Bethmännchen stammen originalgetreu von hier. Auch die Engländer sind richtig auf den Frankfurter Geschmack gekommen. Birmingham zum Beispiel lädt in der Vorweihnachtszeit zum großen "Frankfurt Christmas Market" ein. ✦ Some three million visitors from near and far are drawn to the Frankfurt Christmas Market every year. Santa Claus, twinkling lights and mulled wine ("Glühwein") can be found in other major cities, too, but "Brenten" and "Bethmännchen", the almond cookies Goethe loved so much, are a traditional speciality of Frankfurt. The English have acquired a taste for it, and Birmingham, for example, presents the "Frankfurt Christmas Market" during the holiday season. ✦

URGER
Calamares
POPCORN

# alte oper

Genau genommen ist dieser Prachtbau weder alt noch Oper. 1944 fast vollständig ausgebrannt, konnte das historische Opernhaus mit Bürgerspenden originalgetreu wieder aufgebaut werden. Seit 1981 ist es Konzert- und Kongresszentrum. ✦ To be exact, this magnificent building is neither old nor an opera house. Although in 1944 it was nearly burnt out, the faithful reconstruction of the historic opera house was made possible with donations from citizens. Since 1981 it has been a concert hall and conference centre. ✦

DEM WAHREN SCHOENEN GUTEN.

# die welle

Nicht immer ist die Höhe das Maß aller Dinge, wenn es in der Mainmetropole um innovative architektonische Gestaltung geht. Das CityQuartier "Frankfurter Welle" schlägt eine Brücke zwischen den Wolkenkratzern des Bankenviertels und der im Westend erhaltenen historischen Bebauung. Nur 50 Meter hoch, bietet das "liegende Hochhaus" nahe der Alten Oper viel Platz fürs anspruchsvolle Business, aber auch fürs Wohnen, Einkaufen und Erholen. Die Form der "Welle" ist dem früheren Verlauf des Leerbachs nachempfunden, ein künstlicher Bachlauf nimmt das Motiv in der Promenade wieder auf. ✢

When it comes to innovative architectural structures in the Main-Metropolis, height is not the only criterion. The "Frankfurt Wave" quarter acts as a bridge between the skyscrapers of the banking district and Westend, with its well-preserved historic buildings. The "horizontal skyscraper" near the Alte Oper, only 50 metres tall, offers plenty of space for discriminating businesses, as well as for living, shopping and relaxing. The structure of the Wave recalls the previous course of the Leerbach: this theme is taken up again in the design of the pedestrian area, with its artificial brook. ✢

STARBUCKS COFFEE

# universität

2001 zogen die Geisteswissenschaften ins IG-Farben-Haus ein, bis 2014 soll der Campus Westend zum Herzstück der bislang auf vier Standorte verteilten Goethe-Universität werden. Hier entsteht auch das neue "House of Finance". ✣

In 2001, the faculties for the humanities moved into the I-G-Farben-Haus. By 2014, the Westend Campus should have become the heart of the Goethe-University, hitherto distributed across four locations. The new "House of Finance" will also be built here. ✣

ANG GOETHE-UNIVERSITÄT

# hauptfriedhof

Berühmte und weniger bekannte Frankfurter haben in diesem auf über 70 Hektar würdevoll gestalteten "Landschaftsgarten" seit 1828 die letzte Ruhestätte gefunden. Darunter Nervenarzt Alois Alzheimer und Philosoph Arthur Schopenhauer. +

Famous notables as well as ordinary citizens of Frankfurt have been laid to rest on these seventy hectares of decorously landscaped garden since 1828, among them the neurologist Alois Alzheimer and the philosopher Arthur Schopenhauer. +

# ernst mays "neues frankfurt"

Dezentral, für den kleinen Geldbeutel erschwinglich und der Gesundheit zuträglich: Das waren Standards für die 15.000 innovativen Wohnungen, die Stadtbaurat Ernst May zwischen 1925 und 1930 in Frankfurt schuf. "Vorzeigesiedlung" ist die Römerstadt. ✦

Away from the centre, affordable for those with limited means, and beneficial to their health: those were the standards for the 15,000 apartments that the City Architect Ernst May created in Frankfurt between 1925 and 1930. The Römerstadt is the showplace of this development. ✦

# alter campus bockenheim

Rund 20.000 von 35.000 Studierenden lernen und forschen nach wie vor dort, wo die Wurzeln der Frankfurter Universität liegen - in Bockenheim. Mit dem Ausbau des Campus' Westend wird der Lehrbetrieb hier aber nach und nach eingestellt. ✤

Approximately 20,000 out a total of 35,000 students study and research here as they have always done. This is where the roots of the University of Frankfurt can be found - in Bockenheim. With the expansion of the Westend Campus, the teaching here will be wound down. ✤

U
BOCKENHEIMER WARTE

# senckenbergmuseum

Einmal im Maul eines Finnwals stehen oder mit Urpferd, Dino-Mumie und "Urahn Lucy" den Geheimnissen der Evolution nachforschen: Im grössten Naturkundemuseum Deutschlands ist eine vielfältige Entdeckungsreise über Millionen Jahre möglich. ✤

Stand once in the jaws of a finback whale or investigate the secrets of evolution with the earliest horses, mummies of dinosaurs and your distant ancestor Lucy. In the largest natural history museum in Germany, you can make a multi-faceted voyage of discovery back through millions of years. ✤

# fernmeldeturm

Offiziell heisst er "Europaturm", die Frankfurter nennen ihr mit 337,5 Metern höchstes Bauwerk aber nur "Ginnheimer Spargel". Und das, obwohl es - genau betrachtet - in Bockenheim steht. ✣ Although it is officially named the "Europa Tower", the citizens of Frankfurt call their tallest building, with its 337.5 metres, the "Ginnheimer Spargel" (the stick of asparagus from Ginnheim). And that although it is - strictly speaking - in Bockenheim. ✣

# die akteure

## andrea enderlein

wurde 1958 in Potsdam geboren, arbeitete als Bildredakteurin beim Fernsehen und lebt heute als freie Fotografin im Rhein-Main-Gebiet. Sie ist für Film-Produktionen, TV, Banken und Foto-agenturen im Einsatz - auch redaktionell. Ihre Aufträge führen sie oft nach Frankfurt, z. B. zu Aufnahmen für die Krimi-Serie "Ein Fall für zwei". ✣

## gabi winter

Jahrgang 1960, studierte in Frankfurt Englisch und Germanistik. Nach einem Volontariat war sie mehrere Jahre lang als Lokalredakteurin für eine Frankfurter Tageszeitung tätig. Inzwischen arbeitet sie als freie Journalistin, Redakteurin und Autorin, z. B. für Buchprojekte wie Familien-Ratgeber, Informations- und PR-Broschüren. ✣

## jochen günther

1957 in Rastatt geboren, wuchs in Frankfurt auf und arbeitete hier unter anderem 13 Jahre lang als Redaktionsfotograf für eine renommierte Tageszeitung. Heute ist er - freiberuflich - bundesweit für Illustrierte, Magazine, grosse Firmen, Banken und Agenturen unterwegs, macht Reisereportagen und PR-Aufnahmen. ✣

## fernando baptista

ist als freier Fotograf z. B. für deutschlandweit agierende Tageszeitungen, Magazine, Agenturen und grosse Konzerne tätig. Er kam 1988 über "Zwischenstationen" in Hamburg und Brüssel nach Frankfurt und wirkt hier mittlerweile auch an verschiedenen Buchprojekten mit. Das jüngste: "100 Frankfurter Köpfe". ✣

## norbert hetkamp

Creative Director mit US-Erfahrung, lebt und arbeitet in Frankfurt und auf dem Lande in den Bereichen Editorial-, Grafik-Design und freier Fotografie. Nach dem Design-Studium in Münster und New York City arbeitete er in Hamburg und Frankfurt für Lifestyle-Produkte, heute u.a. für Musikproduzenten und Verlage. ✣

BILDNACHWEIS

ANDREA ENDERLEIN: S. 9/U. L., 10, 11/U., 14, 15/O., 16, 17, 18, 19, 20, 21, 22, 23, 24, 25, 26, 27, 28, 29, 30, 31, 43, 52, 53, 58, 59, 74, 75, 76, 77, 82, 83/O., 85, 86, 87, 88, 89, 94, 96/U., 97, 98/U.L., 104, 105, 106, 107, 118, 119, 120, 121

FERNANDO BAPTISTA: S. 6, 7, 8, 9/O., 9/U.R., 32/U., 34, 35, 36/O., 37/O., 40, 41, 42, 44, 45, 57/O., 62 U., 65 U., 67, 71, 72, 73, 83/U., 84, 90, 91, 92, 93, 95, 96/O., 108, 109, 112/U., 113, 114 U., 115, 122, 123, 124, 125

JOCHEN GÜNTHER: Titel U1, S. 9, 11/O., 12, 13, 15/U., 32/O., 33, 34, 35, 36/U., 37/U., 38, 39, 46, 47, 48, 49, 50, 51, 54, 55, 56, 57/U., 60, 61, 62/O., 63, 64, 65/O., 66, 68, 69, 70, 78, 79, 80, 81, 98/O. 98/U.R., 99, 100, 101, 102, 103, 110, 111, 112/O., 114/O., 116, 117